D0370412

BLAKE E. COHEN, CAP

I LOVE YOU, MORE

SHORT STORIES OF ADDICTION, RECOVERY, AND LOSS
FROM THE FAMILY'S PERSPECTIVE

Copyright© 2019

Blake E. Cohen, CAP

All Rights Reserved

ISBN 13: 978-0-578-50912-9

Printed in the United States of America

LEGAL DISCLAIMER

Addiction and substance use disorders constitute serious health conditions. Treatment requires professional medical care. The information presented in this book is intended to be a guide to help you. Neither the author, nor anyone associated with *I Love You, More* or the information it contains claim that it is a substitute for medical care and/or treatment. Use this book to help you become proactive, ask questions, and discuss treatment options with professional support groups. The author, publisher, or anyone associated with the *I Love You, More* book, website, or any entity under this name are not responsible or liable for any loss or damage allegedly arising from any information or suggestion in the *I Love You, More* book. Our purpose is to educate readers about the toll addiction and substance use disorders take on the family to enable them to live fuller, happier, and healthier lives.

Daria Anne
Media

To my entire family, I would never
be who I am without you.

To my sweetheart Chrissy, thank you for
your undying support and putting up with me.

To those who are still sick and suffering from
the disease of addiction, there is a way out.

To Dan Perry and countless others
we've lost to this disease, you are not forgotten.

BUT FIRST

Imagine the finest cheese to ever be exported from the heart of Italy's rolling hills: perhaps it's gorgonzola...no, it's ricotta ...oh, wait, no, it's Pecorino Romano. Real stinky, salty goodness featuring a subtle, delightful crunch of flavor when you bite into it. Now, imagine someone has placed a tantalizing slice of this Italian delicacy onto a mouse trap, enticing any small rodent to its untimely death as it follows its nose to the source of this irresistible aroma and the satisfaction it promises.

Our unsuspecting rodent – though susceptible to being crushed into oblivion – cannot resist the allure of what is certain to bring him instant pleasure. As the intoxicating scent leads him into the deadly metal contraption upon which the aged pile of hardened sheep's milk rests, he recognizes the trap. In fact, our tiny mouse has watched in horror while many of his friends perished at the mercy of similar devices.

Yet the olfactory allure of the cheese tricks him into believing he can outsmart the deathtrap; contending with it for the ultimate prize is worth the risk of possibly taking a one-way trip to mousey heaven.

Indeed, his animal urge to devour the seductive cheese

blend is too strong: he decides to ignore the perils and go in for "just a tiny nibble." He inches towards the cheese, getting close enough to take a small bite and – wow! It's everything he hoped it would be. Salty, but smooth; firm, yet sharp and smoky.

Maybe he should take one more bite? Never has he experienced such remarkable ecstasy: what's the harm in savoring just one more, tiny, little taste? As the mouse moves his snout closer to the cheese, he closes his eyes and wraps his mouth around it, salivating over the next rush of flavor when, SLAM! The steel bar of the trap crushes his tiny body in a fatal blow...and for what? For a few fleeting moments of cheesy pleasure, our mouse sacrificed his life. Was it worth it?

That is addiction.

Pain medications. Anxiety medications. Heroin. Cocaine. Alcohol. Uppers. Downers. Poppers. Synthetics.

Like the allure of cheese to a mouse, these substances make so many false promises of untold pleasure to a human being that even when fully aware of the dangers, they are willing to risk their freedom, their family, and even their lives for just a small taste of temporary pleasure. Over and over again.

-Blake E. Cohen, CAP
Certified Addictions Professional

For Updates and More Information from the Author, Please Visit: <u>BlakeEvanCohen.com</u>

FOREWORD

I did not witness Blake in the grips of his addiction. I did not see the impact that his use had on his family. By the time I met Blake he had already wrestled with his demons, went to treatment multiple times, and met our facility's unwritten minimal standard of two years' sustained abstinence and active maintenance of a recovery program. It was, and continues to be, our ideology that an individual must heal oneself before attempting to help others. It is easy to be judgmental, consider addiction to be driven by moral failure, and not a true illness. But it is extremely hard to be open-minded, consider the thoughts and feelings of others, and to make individual change. What has always impressed me about Blake is that he seems to deeply understand this concept. He consistently strives for personal growth, and in doing so, has helped many others.

I was the CEO of the treatment facility in which Blake sought employment and entry into the substance abuse field. Although he already had experience in marketing, as well as treatment of those with severe mental health disorders, Blake was humble and willing to start as a Behavioral Health Technician rather than the Admissions Director position he had pursued. He was also seemingly unaffected by the significant pay differential between the two roles. In the interview that day he told me that he looked at it as an opportunity towards personal development and understanding of others.

Blake immediately embraced the BHT role in much the same way I have witnessed him encounter everything he does. He enmeshed himself entirely into the process, genuinely listened to every patient or staff member he encountered, and eagerly learned everything available about the job and more. In a relatively short amount of time, he had a unique understanding of the patient encounter inside our treatment facility and was promoted to the Director of Admissions. His personal experience with addiction, unwavering empathy, and intelligence soon turned him into the best Admissions Director I had worked with in twenty-five years in behavioral health.

Blake poured his entire being into the position. In doing so, he spent thousands of hours with desperate and struggling individuals and their families during the most profoundly disturbing periods of their lives. He cried with them, mourned their losses, and witnessed true and sustained miracles of recovery. I was in his office one day when the mother of an individual who had overdosed sent him a necklace bearing the ashes of her deceased son. The connection he had made in attempting to assist this individual and his family was genuine, unique, and never to be forgotten. Neither past, nor present employment have been perceived as a job for Blake, but rather an opportunity to give back and help others to become well.

Although fictional, the stories within this book do not stray from the daily experiences that Blake has had a window into. Stories of loss, tragedy, trauma and recovery are being experienced across America and the world daily. Most individuals receive no handbook on how to best address the substance use disorder of oneself or a loved one. Most families do not know where to turn for support and guidance when a child, parent, or spouse becomes ill. Society offers little to educate the public or de-stigmatize the problem of drug addiction.

The compulsion to use substances tends to drain every ounce of life from the individual, but this is even more true for family members. Among many other more complicated factors, during active use getting high serves to self-medicate and block out the implications of one's actions upon others. Family members rarely have any such relief and their loved one's use conversely causes them greater pain. While patients receive a respite upon entering treatment or even incarceration, family members continue to be distraught by overwhelming hardship and intense unrelenting anguish. The consequences of addiction can be severe and sustained long after the acute stage. It is extremely difficult not to get lost in the process; and even more difficult to understand what the other person is thinking, feeling, and experiencing. Stories like the ones Blake tells within *I Love You More* are imperative to promote greater understanding of all sides of the toll drug and alcohol addiction take.

Jeffrey Huttman, Ph.D.
Licensed Psychologist

INTRODUCTION

Allow me to begin by telling you what this book isn't.

This book isn't another personal account of finding redemption after battling the turmoil of addiction. This book isn't a nonfiction, historical piece chronicling the nation's battle with the drug epidemic, though as of its publication, drugs remain the number one cause of accidental death throughout the United States. It isn't another exposé into the rampant corruption of the pharmaceutical industry or the pharmaceutical companies that are so often promoted and glorified on the nightly news. Nor is it a feel-good story of false hope, an opinionated piece on where we are failing as a country, or a solution to scoring a victory in the war on drugs. If you are looking for any of the above, you may end up disappointed by the time you reach the end.

Now that I've shared what this book is NOT about, what is its purpose? It is meant to be an emotional education on the family systems affected by addiction utilizing three, fictional short stories, all with very different endings. And while each of the story's conclusions may vary, they all contain some common threads: hope, pain, mistrust, trust, grief, change, acceptance, worry, and the constant presence of varying levels of sanity across a broad spectrum.

So now that I've told you the what, allow me to tell you the who and why.

My name is Blake, and I'm an alcoholic and an addict in long-term recovery. I have a bachelor's degree in psychology, as proven by the framed document hanging on my office wall – the one that was mailed to me because I missed my graduation ceremony honoring my achievement. Why? I was in a treatment center at the time. A couple of treatments later, I found recovery from my own demons and returned to school to earn a state certification in addiction. According to the Florida Certification Board, I am now a Certified Addictions Professional. I often poke fun at my state-sanctioned title, not because it isn't legitimate or significant, but because much of what I learned in these accreditation courses I had already experienced for myself in real life – whether from my own active addiction habits or the previous year of work I'd completed in the field of substance abuse treatment prior to completing the fourteen-month certification course. Nonetheless, I have letters following my name and for that, my ego is stroked. Speaking of ego-stroking, I needed a 78 to pass the state exam but failed my first attempt by one point. However, growing up in a family surrounded by attorneys, I learned to never go down without a fight. I argued to the board that one of their questions was flawed; therefore, I deserved the one point that caused my failure. When they found my dispute to be accurate and awarded me my certification via diploma, I was elated. To this day, I stand by my argument.

Combined with what I already knew, studying for this certification helped open my eyes to new perspectives I hadn't yet come to understand. We had hours of ethics training – something I believe should be required of every employee in the field of substance abuse treatment – which helped me understand the difference between my own personal recovery program and what it means to be employed by a facility that treats mental and behavioral health issues. I developed a further understanding of the biological side of addiction, learning why addiction is considered a brain disease by medical professionals. Most importantly, I received in-depth training on the family systems and the impact the substance abuser makes on their family, and vice-versa.

It was as if somebody placed a new set of glasses over my eyes. Now, I did develop an understanding early on, at the most basic level, that my own personal addiction was negatively impacting my loved one's lives, but I never truly grasped what it must have been like from their perspective. I think the reverse is also true; that it was likewise difficult for them to grasp what it was like from my perspective during my active addiction and even afterwards.

In the ensuing years after earning my CAP, I began to pay close attention to the family dynamics at play within our patients' lives as we treated them. My jobs in the treatment field as Director of Admissions and National Outreach Manager involved guiding and coaching the family and the person struggling towards entering treatment through this tough time of transition. I'm not sure if it's true for everyone in these positions or just my personality, but I tend to form strong bonds with those I'm trying to assist. This has led to the development of many incredible relationships that I cherish to this day.

Paying close attention to how a family is affected, I've witnessed a wide array of emotional responses to coping with a loved one who is addicted to substances. I've seen those who try to educate themselves and those who have dumped their loved ones off on a curb, wanting nothing to do with them anymore. I've watched loved ones take the drugs themselves to try to understand how the pull of something inanimate could be so strong. I've listened to crying grandparents beg for their "real" grandchild to come back to them. I've witnessed frustration levels beyond my comprehension. I've received phone calls from mothers, informing me with chilling calmness in their voice, that they just found their son passed away on the couch from an overdose.

What I've rarely seen, though, is genuine understanding of the other person's side of the story. But it's not for a lack of trying. Many families I've worked with have attended family weekend programming, joined local support groups, and purchased books on addiction. However, what I am referring to is the act of truly placing themselves within the bodies of their loved ones to view the world from their perspective. A feat, I understand, to be terribly difficult to accomplish.

I Love You, More offers insight into the various perspectives and experiences of family members who have dealt with the harrowing disease of addiction. The goal of this book is to be the conduit that allows you to enter the body and mind of an addict and their family, to see the world through their eyes as they navigate their way through one of the most tumultuous, heart-breaking, and gut-wrenching hardships they will ever face.

From mothers to fathers to siblings to the struggling individual themselves, I've created three easy-to-read stories that chronicle each family member's emotional understanding of the situation. Although these stories are fictional, they are comprised of countless tidbits from my years in the treatment field speaking with families. Using my experiences, the experiences of others, and information obtained from interviews I've conducted, they include a story of recovery from addiction; a story of a young man who can't stop himself from using despite the dire consequences he's facing; and a tale of grief after losing a child to an overdose.

One can never truly understand another person's life or decisions unless they've spent time in that person's shoes – walking the proverbial mile of their experiences. I hope this book offers you a new understanding – whether you are a family member, the person suffering from a substance use disorder, or just someone interested in learning more about the intricacies of the disease of addiction. This book is addressed to you, whoever you are, as an opportunity to embody a day in the life of someone living with a disease that affects millions.

There is no cure for addiction. There is no magic pill that can make it all go away, in fact, a "magic pill" just may be the reason a person struggling with a substance use disorder is in the situation they're in. The most we can do to help resolve this growing epidemic is to offer education and insight into the disease of addiction. We can spread understanding and reduce the stigma surrounding substance use disorders. People are quick to judge those in the grips of addiction; it is a silent killer that often lies unnoticed without proper training. Allow this book to serve as an educational resource for you. A metaphorical new pair of glasses; a tool to change the way you see addiction to enable you to approach those who suffer from the disease of addition with compassion, instead of confusion, disgust or dismay.

After you read the stories, I recommend reading through the discussion questions at the end. They will help to expand your perspective and tie the stories together while guiding your understanding of the experiences each character undergoes. Since they are designed to make you think, please don't skip over them. It may also be of interest to read the stories aloud or together in a group setting, then use the questions to facilitate productive conversations. The stories and questions can all be read consecutively or separately, depending on how the reader chooses to use this book. There is no right or wrong way to read it.

I hope you enjoy *I Love You, More* and that it serves you in whichever way you need it to.

STORY ONE

RECOVERY

PART 1

"JOSH, how many times do I have to tell you: I want every single bottle in the medicine cabinet brought out to the kitchen table one more time! Dad's about to get home and the discharge planner at the rehab said we need to get rid of anything that's abusable or could trigger him." From his comfy place on the couch, Josh looks toward his mom in the kitchen and rolls his eyes. As he gets up, he pauses the television and buries the remote in the back pocket of his pants before making his way out of the living room and into the master bathroom.

It's been 44 days since his dad, Roman, left for rehab for the third time – and the tension caused by his pending arrival has the entire family on edge. Even their dog, Einstein, senses something is going on, as evidenced by his anxious pacing around the house all afternoon.

"Okay, this is everything. I checked all the labels and I don't see a single medication that was on the list they sent us," Josh announces confidently. "I'm pretty sure you threw everything out the last time he left anyway and, literally, every one of his doctors hates us because of how many times you've called them to warn them he's an addict." Shelly stares at her 17-year-old son, in a way that only a mother could, that completely shuts him up and compels him to quietly put the medications down on the counter, pull the TV remote out of his back pocket, and walk back over to the couch. He lifts the remote towards the screen to hit the "play" button, but before he does, he quietly mumbles to himself: "It's not like this rehab was any different than from the last two times he's gone, anyway. Dad is Dad. He's not going to change."

The matriarch of the family and the sturdy rock that keeps the household from collapsing, Shelly examines the pill bottles Josh brought to the kitchen. In silence, she feverishly glances back and forth from each bottle to a list she has printed out entitled "Medications to Avoid in Early Recovery." Even though she memorized the list and recognizes most of the medications from the discharge instructions she received from her husband's last treatment center, she wants to make sure she didn't miss anything.

"Oh my God, the vitamin bottles. Josh, you didn't bring me the bottles of vitamins that were in there!" she screams towards the other room.

With a confused look smacked across his face, Josh yells back, "Mom, I'm pretty sure you can't get high on vitamin C!"

Shelly debates whether to tell her son the truth about finding pain medication his father had hidden in a bottle of multi-vitamins a couple months ago. After a brief pause, she realizes some things are better left unsaid and commands, "Josh, just get me the damn bottles!" In recent years, her parenting style has become a balancing act of being truthful with her son about his father's addiction in the hope it will deter him from embarking upon his own "experimental phase," and salvaging what's left of their relationship. After all, Roman is still Josh's father and she doesn't want to ruin their chances of rebuilding the closeness and trust they once shared.

"Jesus, Mom. I'll get the vitamins, you weirdo."

PART 2

As Roman's Uber pulls into the driveway, the dog's head pops up with his ears standing at attention.

"Holy sh...crap! He's here!" Shelly exclaims as her eyes dart around the room in search of something she may have forgotten in preparation for his arrival.

"Mom, relax. You're already annoying me, and he hasn't even walked in yet," Josh remarks.

As the car door slams shut, the dog goes wild, scratching and whining at the front door in anticipation. "I'm going to my room. Have fun pretending like he's not coming back from rehab for the third time," Josh announces. With that, he gets off the couch and proceeds down the hallway.

The noise of Roman's key turning in the lock-hole causes Shelly's stomach to drop to her feet as a tidal wave of anxious thoughts floods her mind:

"Is this time really going to be different?"

"What if he fails? What happens then?"

"I can't put Josh through this again."

"He won't survive another relapse."

"We won't survive another one."

"I can't put my --"

A sudden realization interrupts the barrage of negative thoughts assaulting her mind: I changed the locks last week! Shelly lunges forward to unlock the door. As it swings open, Einstein bombards Roman with the kind of unconditional love all dog owners know and appreciate. After a lovefest lasting about a minute or two, Einstein runs back inside and Roman takes his first steps into the foyer, inhaling deeply through his nose to breathe in the familiar scent of home.

Then his eyes settle on his anxious wife standing in front of him with her arms crossed. "Hello, sweetheart," he says in a soft voice. With hesitancy, Shelly moves in closer to Roman and places her hands on either side of his face. Examining his rejuvenated, healthy-looking complexion, her eyes well up with tears, "You look so much better. You look like my Ro again."

Roman's first instinct is to launch into an apology for what transpired before he went away again but he stops himself and decides to simply appreciate this moment with his wife. As he hugs her, he realizes his addiction has taken an immeasurable emotional toll on her and Josh. No matter how much he wants to explain his seriousness about his recovery this time, he knows his words will fall on deaf ears. He acknowledges that the only way to prove it to them is by showing them that he's willing to put in the time and effort to change. Phrases like "I'm sorry" or "It won't happen again" have lost their meaning in this household. This time, he is going to have to earn back their trust.

PART 3

Josh closes the door to his bedroom behind him, rolls his eyes at Einstein's whimpers to let him in, and puts a pair of earbuds in his ears. He opens the messaging app on his phone and starts a new text thread with his best friend, Zach:

Josh: Yo, guess who's back from the loony bin?

Zach: lol Waddap!? Pops make his big return today, huh?

Josh: It's so annoying, dude. My mom acts like nothing happened. Guess she magically goes blind whenever she walks past the broken patio door frame he kicked open two months ago.

Zach: Daayum! That still ain't fixed?!!

Josh: Lol sort of. Our neighbor came over and kinda put it back together, but it still looks wrecked AF.

Zach: Did you see him yet? What's he look like? Did he try to make you pray with him like last time? Lol

Josh: Nope. I came to my room and shut the door when I heard him pull up. I think he just walked in the house. Bet my mom's already crying lol

Zach: She's crying? Why?

Josh: I dunno, man.

Zach: Alright, man. G-Luck with that. I gotta get back to work before my boss freaks again.

Josh: Ya...thx. Later, dude.

"Josh, come say hi to your dad!" Shelly calls from the other room. He pretends like he couldn't hear it and cranks up the volume on his music, shaking his head and laughing to himself, "No, thanks."

PART 4

"Josh, come say hi to your dad!" Shelly repeats with more urgency, loud enough for him to hear in the other room. She glances toward his bedroom in anticipation of a response, then back at her husband. When still no answer comes, she opens her mouth to yell even louder, but Roman stops her. "Honey let's give him some space," he suggests in a calm voice.

Unsatisfied and nervous that Roman may become agitated, Shelly takes a few steps in Josh's direction, then turns around after giving it some more thought. "Um, maybe, you're right." She offers him an awkward smile. "You should know, though, he's happy you're back. He's just being a teenager and doing what teenagers do best...ignoring their parents."

Laughing in agreement, Roman uses his thumb to point to the window behind him. "Help me get the rest of my stuff from driveway?" Shelly nods and they both begin walking out the front door. "I think that Uber driver was having stomach issues, by the way. I had to ride the whole way here with my head halfway out the window," he jokes, attempting to coax a smile from his distraught wife.

They both pick up a bag and make their way back inside the house, where Roman begins to describe his latest treatment experience; anything to break the silence and ignore the discomfort they both feel. "You should have seen how my unit was set up! It was four to a bedroom, which also meant four to a bathroom. Just imagine that for a second: four gross guys, coming off God-knows-what drug, forced to share a bathroom. There was almost a fight every morning over whose job it was to clean it that day," he grins as he reminisces about the experience, while Shelly does her best to focus on his words and ignore the drumbeat in her chest.

"Speaking of cleaning, every morning we all had chores to finish before we could get breakfast. This wasn't like the last cushy rehab I was in where we had a maid service. Nope. We had to clean everything ourselves or else face the consequences." He shakes his head and laughs, "Can you imagine me cleaning? I do have to say, though, it was exactly what I think I needed."

To keep the conversation flowing, Shelly remarks, "Sounds like the staff was pretty tough on you guys."

"Yeah, I guess so but I kind of liked that they didn't baby us. My therapist was also a no bullshit kind of guy. One night, before bed, he –"

Shelly cuts off Roman in mid-sentence, "Oh my God, that reminds me; we were supposed to call that therapist they recommended right away!"

"I already did. Called in the Uber," Roman responds, with a proud smile on his face.

"You already called?" With a look of disbelief stemming from a long history of lies and deception, Shelly gazes at her husband with skepticism and concern. "You spoke to him?"

"Yep, look, I'll show you on my phone." With that, he provides his wife visual proof of his four-minute, 26-second phone call to the number that matches the one she'd jotted down on a notepad.

"I'm sorry, Ro. I didn't mean to question you. It's just that --" Roman grabs her hand and Shelly stops speaking.

"You've got every right to question me. I've earned it. In fact, I've earned it many times over. You and Josh have been tormented by me repeatedly. I've lied to you, manipulated you, and given you every reason not to trust me." He lets go of her hands and looks down towards the floor, "Those damn pills blew up my life and you both caught all the shrapnel. I know that I can never say 'sorry' enough times to make up for any of the pain I've caused either of you. I'm not going to make any promises to you that I can't keep or tell you that none of what happened before couldn't happen again. I'm just going to do my best, one day at a time, to avoid repeating those same mistakes again."

Shelly stares at her husband and tries to process his words. She likes what she is hearing, but with a history like theirs, she can't help but be skeptical of such grandiose speeches, especially since she's heard them all before.

"Okay, Ro. We'll see." She moves towards the refrigerator and reaches for the handle. "You've been traveling all day. You must be starving. I'll make you some dinner." She searches around for something she can cook and realizes that in the middle of all the chaos surrounding his return, she forgot to go grocery shopping. She slowly stands back up, closes the refrigerator door, and looks at her husband, "What do you say we go out to eat?"

"You know what? I called Darin on the way here and we talked about going to a meeting tonight, if that's okay with you?" Surprised by his response, Shelly doesn't know how to answer and just stares at him for a moment.

"I mean, I don't have to go, but the rehab suggested I should hit a meeting right away when I got home, so I thought I would. If you don't want me to, I won't," he says, worried about upsetting her.

"No, oh my God, I'm sorry. Absolutely, if that's what you want to do then you should go."

"Well, then I will." Roman smiles again and envelopes her in another warm embrace. With his arms still wrapped around her, he pulls his head back to look her in the eye, "you forgot to go grocery shopping, didn't you?"

PART 5

ROMAN WALKS into the house around 8:15 p.m. and throws his keys onto the side table next to the front door. Josh is sitting on the couch, watching TV in the living room when his father walks in. Before noticing his son's presence, Roman turns and waves at his sponsor Darin as he drives away. Because he wants to avoid direct contact with his father, Josh quickly turns off the TV and heads back to the sanctuary of his room.

"Hey Josh," Roman greets him in a soft voice. It's the first time he's seen him since he's gotten home from treatment only a few hours earlier.

"Hi. Bye," Josh replies with attitude as he continues walking to his destination.

Roman reaches out his hand and takes a few tentative steps in his son's direction. "Dude, wait up." Josh stops, his back facing his father, and heaves a frustrated sigh.

"What, Dad?"

"Nothing, I just want to talk to you. I just got home from a meeting and --"

"Oh, let me guess," Josh interrupts in a derisive tone, "you went to a meeting and now everything is going to be fine, right?"

He turns around to look into Roman's eyes, his face red with anger, "I'm not Mom. I'm not going to pretend that everything that's happened – everything you've done – didn't happen." He moves in closer to his father with his chest puffed out, looking more like a man than a teenager, "You get to go away while I'm the one who has to stay here and watch Mom cry every day. I'm the one that's stuck here cleaning up your mess with her while you sit in your little therapy sessions talking about how you are the one with all the problems!"

Taken aback by the outburst, Roman tries to remain calm and reason with his son, "Josh, I know and --"

"You know what, Dad, save it for someone else who buys into your bullshit!" Josh turns on his heel and storms into his bedroom, slamming the door so hard that the whole house shakes.

Awakened by her son's screams, Shelly rushes to the living room to find her husband standing there alone. "What's going on in here? Why is he yelling?" she asks, holding her hands at her sides in a gesture of confusion. Unsure of how to respond, Roman remains silent and frozen in place while his eyes dart back and forth between his wife's face and his son's door. Before Shelly can say anything else, he turns around, snatches his house keys from the table by the foyer, and swings the front door open.

"Screw it." Roman grabs the car keys and rushes out of the house, slamming the door behind him. Dumbfounded, Shelly stares wide-eyed into space, alone in the living room, and hears the screech of tires down the driveway as her husband pulls away from the house, bound for God-only-knows where.

ONE YEAR LATER

"Jesus, Josh; put your phone down for two freaking seconds and do what I told you! Dad is going to be home any minute and everything needs to be ready!"

"Mom, you really need to see a psychiatrist or something. You're losing your mind!" Notwithstanding his snappy comment, Josh obliges his mother and makes his way into the kitchen, where he raises his arms in confusion and asks, "What do you need me to do? Seriously, I think we've covered everything. The house is ready for when he gets here."

Einstein pops his head up in seeming agreement before laying it back down next to his food bowl, one of his favorite spots. Shelly gives the room a quick scan with her eyes, then walks towards the doorway to poke her head into the living room to confirm Josh is right before returning to the kitchen counter.

"When did they say he's supposed to be dropped off?" she asks aloud, giving voice to her tortured thoughts. She eagerly glances at her watch and then over to the clock on the microwave as if making sure the time on her watch was correct. "He should be here any minute, I think."

Josh approaches his mother and grabs her playfully by her shoulders. "Seriously, relax. You're making *me* want to do drugs."

"Josh, that's not even close to funny!" she yells as he runs out of the kitchen snickering. Just as he sits down on the couch, they hear a car pulling up to the driveway. Josh jumps back up and Shelly shrieks, "Oh, he's here!"

The two of them look at each other, as if expecting the other person to instruct them on what to do next. Then in the following moment, mother and son simultaneously rush toward the kitchen doorway. Einstein runs in the opposite direction, bound for the front door, where he slams right into Josh's legs, causing him to make a tumbling entrance into the kitchen.

For some reason, the sound of the key turning in the lock seems much louder than usual to Shelly and Josh as they wait in breathless anticipation. When they hear the crunch of tires backing out of the driveway, their hearts begin to pound. The door opens and Roman takes a few slow steps into the foyer. He notices that the house feels eerily calm and he pivots his head around, looking for signs of life.

"Shell? Josh? You here?"

Shelly forces herself to answer, "We're in the kitchen," in the most serious tone she can muster.

"Okay...is everything alright?" Roman asks as he begins to move in their direction. "You sound weird." Roman turns the corner to find his wife and son standing beside the kitchen counter bearing a cake decorated with a lit "1" candle. He watches as the flame from the candle dances in the cool breeze blowing out of the air-conditioner.

"Surprise!" Shelly and Josh exclaim in unison.

"We're so proud of you; celebrating one year sober is a huge deal!" his wife declares, beaming with pride as she gazes at her husband. With an enormous grin on his face, Roman reaches into his pocket.

"So, I'm guessing you guys want to see it, huh?"

With that, he pulls out something small and gold-colored and tosses it to Josh, who catches it before slowly opening his hand to look at it. Then he reads the inscription on the coin aloud:

"One. To Thine Own Self Be True."

Josh hands it to Shelly and embraces his father. "Proud of you, Dad," he whispers, before taking a few steps back.

"Thanks, bud. I'm proud of you both too. I couldn't have done it without you guys." Roman moves in to give his son another hug, then offers him a big smile, "Plus, you're going away to college tomorrow; we've got to celebrate that too! This cake isn't just for me, it's for all of us."

Josh looks over at his mother, "Mom, are you crying again?"

"Shut up," she laughs, dabbing her eyes with a paper towel. "Leave me alone."

Roman takes a few steps back, a serious expression forming on his face. "Would you all want to say a quick prayer together?" The three of them exchange glances, then burst out in simultaneous laughter.

"I love you, Dad, but that was a weird period of our lives I'd like to forget ever happened!" Josh replies as he embraces his father again. In the next moment, they extend their arms towards a weeping Shelly with a gleeful laugh, "Come here, Mom. We know you want to."

When the realization hits Josh that he's engaged in a group hug with his parents, he breaks away and heads back to the kitchen counter. "Alright, enough of this sentimental crap. Who's cutting the cake?"

PART 7

JOSH IS LYING on his bed for the last time before going away to college, listening to music through his earbuds as he mindlessly peruses his Instagram feed. Roman knocks softly on the slightly ajar door before slowly pushing it open and peeking his head into his son's room.

"Can I come in?" he asks in a soft voice.

Josh notices his dad's face in the doorway and pulls out one of his earbuds. "What?"

"I said, can I come in?"

"Yeah, sure. What's up?" Josh asks as he adjusts himself to a seated position on the bed.

"What are you listening to?"

"Do you remember that playlist of 'our' songs I made for your iPod before you went away the first time a few years ago?"

Roman nods with wide eyes, "Yep, I'm pretty sure that's what got me through my first treatment center. Without that music, I would have missed you guys way too much and never made it to the end. It's all the songs that we listened to together throughout your whole life. I couldn't believe you remembered to put some of them on there; a few of them we hadn't listened to since you were just a little kid."

Josh turns his phone around to show his dad the same playlist. "Well, that's what I'm listening to right now. I've had it saved on my phone this whole time and leaving for college tomorrow, and all, I just feel weird. These songs take me back to a lot of happy times we shared together as a family." He scrolls through the playlist with his thumb. "I've never been so far from both you and mom at the same time so I'm just feeling a little freaked out, or whatever." Wanting to maintain a tough demeanor in front of his dad, he stops talking as he feels the tears bubbling up in his eyes. Roman sits on the edge of his bed and pats his son's feet underneath the covers.

"We're going to miss you too, buddy," he assures him as he gazes around the room. Then he looks into his eyes and says, "There's something I wanted to tell you before you left. I've been wanting to tell you this since I got home a year ago, but I knew I needed to wait until you'd actually want to hear me say it." Concerned, Josh sits up straighter, removes the second earbud, and leans his back against the headboard.

Roman continues, "All those years, while I was out there doing whatever it was that I was doing, I wasn't being the father I should have been to you. I don't remember any of your first days of high school. I missed all your debate meetings. I can't even tell you the name of your first girlfriend that I vaguely remember you bringing home for dinner, once. I don't think, between 9th and 11th grade, I ever helped you with homework or, even helped teach you how to drive. Mom had to be your mother and your father and God knows that woman is capable of anything.

"Every day, I'd think to myself 'tomorrow will be the day that I clean up my act and I'll take Josh to school. Tomorrow, I'll be his dad.' It took so many 'tomorrows' for me to finally get to a point where I stopped even trying to convince myself that I could be there to take you to school the next day.

"I'm saying all this to say, I don't want you to think, for one second, that you ever meant any less to me. You are the thing that makes me the proudest in this world. I can't even believe you've turned out to be as incredible as you have, and I've got your mom mostly to thank for that." Roman pauses to shift his body closer. "It may have seemed like I cared about those drugs more than you, but I want you to really know, to fully understand, that's just not the case. You always have, and always will, mean the world to me. I may not have been there for you the past few years like I should have been, but I am going to try my damn hardest to be there for you in the coming years and beyond."

Roman gives Josh an assuring smile, "I'll always have your back, kid. No matter how far you are from us, I'm just one phone call away." With that, he pats his foot again, takes a deep breath, looks over at Josh's packed bags, and just grins. Shaking his head in disbelief and pride over everything his only child has become, he settles his eyes on his face and says "I love you, Josh."

Listening intently, Josh blinks a few times to prevent any tears from escaping his eyes. He is still too much off a stubborn teenager to let his dad see him cry, so he grabs his earbuds and puts them back in. But before he hits 'play,' he looks at his dad with a slight smirk on his face and says:

"I love you, more."

STORY TWO

PART 1

8:33 a.m. Tweet by @GabiGabberz94 "My brother's sentencing is today. Literally, would rather be going anywhere else. SMH"

GABI PUTS her phone down on her dresser and walks over to the full-length mirror on the back of her bedroom door to take another look at her court outfit. Realizing the wrinkles on her shirt didn't fall out the way she was hoping they would, she tries to smooth them with her hand but then notices something even more alarming – a white toothpaste stain on her collar. She leans in to get a better look.

KNOCK. KNOCK. KNOCK.

Gabi jumps back, startled by the knocking on the door. "Let's go, Gabs. Dad is already in the car waiting for us!" a voice on the other side yells. Gabi gives herself one more glance in the mirror, rubs the toothpaste stain with her finger, lets out a frustrated exhale, and responds, "Coming!" As she opens the door to walk out, she pauses to grab her phone off the dresser.

She meets her mom, Gladys, in the hallway and together, they head towards the front door. "You ready to go?" Gladys asks.

"No, but it's not like I have a choice."

Gladys weaves her arm through her daughter's arm, and they continue walking to the car. Noticing the agitated expression on her husband's face as he sits in in the driver's seat, Gladys picks up the pace, pulling Gabi along with her until they reach the front and back passenger doors. Gladys sits up front next to her husband while Gabi hops into the seat directly behind her mother.

"It's about damn time! Where the hell were you two?" barks Joel. "Marco's sentencing hearing is at 9:30 and thanks to both of you, we're going to be late!"

"Okay, Joel, we are here now. Let's just go and get this over with." In an unmistakable display of annoyance, he gives his wife the side-eye before throwing the car into reverse and backing out of the driveway. Gabi reaches into her purse and pulls out her phone.

8:37 a.m. Tweet by @GabiGabberz94
"Two seconds into our car ride and the 'rents are already fighting. SMH x2"

PART 2

IN THE BACK SEAT, Gabi tries to take her mind off her nervous stomach by staring out the window on this cold, drab winter day. Being a couple weeks into the New Year, she takes a mental note of which houses still have Christmas decorations on the lawn in an attempt to distract herself from the reality she is going to have to face in just a short while: after today, her brother won't be seeing anything other than the inside of a prison cell for a very long time.

Up in the front seat, her parents resume their argument from the night before. The tension in the car is so palpable it almost feels sticky. Gabi shifts her attention from the window to her mom, who is waving her hands in the air as she fights with her dad.

"You gave up on him months ago! He is our son. Our son! There is more that we could have done, but now, because you refused to pay for that lawyer my sister recommended, we have to go watch our son get hauled off to jail!"

Joel grips the steering wheel tighter and bites his lip. The tension in the car rises to an unbearable level and prevents Gabi from focusing on anything other than her mom and dad's verbal sparring match. Gladys fumes, "You don't just give up on a person! We could have helped him more. So what? He fucked up!" Joel reacts by rapping the wheel even harder with the pads of his fingers and pursing his lips tighter. "People make mistakes, but we are his family," Gladys continues. "He needs to know his family is always there for him no matter what! We could help him, we just needed to try --"

Joel erupts, "Help him! People make mistakes?! Are you hearing yourself!" The sheer volume of her father's screams pierces her eardrums and causes Gabi to wince in the back seat. "How many God damn times have we already been through this? Huh? How many times?!" Too scared to reply to her husband's rhetorical question, Gladys remains silent, shifts in her seat, and folds her arms.

"You can't help people who don't want to be helped! We sent him to rehab six times! Six! We were insane after two times, but we kept spending money to send him away anyway, like idiots!" Joel points in the direction of the county jail where his son is awaiting trial. "Marco doesn't give a shit about us! We are his punching bags, his bank accounts, his babysitters, and suppliers for every damn pawn shop in town!" He punches the steering wheel in frustration before pausing to take a deep, calming breath. After he exhales, he proceeds to speak in a tone that can only be described as one of total defeat. "I'm done. Okay?" He looks at his wife, seated next to him, "We have to be done. We are just as much at fault as he is at this point. I can't watch him kill himself anymore, so frankly, I'm glad to watch the judge sentence him to time in jail today. At least I know if he's behind bars that he's somewhere safe, where people are watching him."

Gladys doesn't say a word. A stubborn, prideful woman who hates to admit when she's wrong, in her heart, she knows her husband is right this time. Gabi wants so desperately to say something to make her parents feel better, but the right words aren't coming to mind. Instead, she decides to pretend as if she doesn't exist for the remaining 15-minute ride to the courthouse and goes back to staring out the window in silence. It's nothing new for her, anyway. Gabi is used to disappearing into a theoretical non-existence, the result of years of watching her brother drain away her parents' attention, time, energy, and money.

"We'll be there soon," Joel announces as he pushes the power button on the radio with more force than necessary. The mindless droning of a political talk show provides momentary relief from the palpable tension and silence...that is, until the moment the car pulls into the courthouse parking lot, spiking renewed anxiety and apprehension in all three of its passengers.

PART 3

JUDGE HARRIS GLANCES around the room, then down at the papers in front of him. As he taps his fingers on the stand, it is obvious he is deeply troubled by the decision he must make. "Before I go forth with sentencing, Mr. Juarez, do you have anything you'd like to say?" he asks his defendant.

Marco Juarez's family is seated four rows back, behind the defense's table. Gladys looks at her husband, sitting straight up on the edge of his seat and reaches out to grab his hand. Although it is moist with nervous sweat, she barely notices. Gabi sits on the other side of her mother, gnawing at her nails and bouncing her leg in anxious anticipation. Instinctively, she scoots closer for maternal comfort as they await her brother's reply to the judge's question.

Marco appears as if he is about to speak but stops and looks at his court-appointed attorney for approval. However, the public defender assigned to his case is too busy shuffling the papers in front of her to pay any attention to him, so he takes a deep breath and utters, "No, your honor. I have nothing to say," in a voice devoid of emotion.

His mother hangs her head and lets go of her husband's

hand to wipe away a tear that has trickled out from her watery eyes. Even amid the turmoil of her son's sentencing, she remains true to herself and salvages her eye-makeup before a tearful outburst can ruin it. Her husband, on the other hand, doesn't flinch. Like a statue, he remains frozen in place on the edge of the hardwood pew, his eyes fixed on the back of his son's head.

The judge's forehead furrows from his eyebrows pulling together as he begins to speak. "Son, you have made three appearances in this court in the past eighteen months and in those appearances, have gotten off relatively easy." Judge Harris commands both Marco and his attorney's full attention now as they stand in preparation for what he is about to say next.

"Your attorney and family have attributed your crimes to your substance use disorders, and I have taken that into careful consideration throughout your career as a criminal." Judge Harris removes his glasses and places them on the podium in front of him. "This time, however, you have shown the court that you are incapable of learning from your mistakes and have made little-to-no effort to reform your behavior. While I firmly grasp the gravity of your addiction, I also believe that one must be held accountable for their actions."

Marco's hand begins to tremble. The agonizing realization that he may not be going home any time soon runs rampant through his mind. A few rows behind him, Gladys, Joel, and Gabi are trying their best maintain a calm, steady demeanor while the Judge lays out his sentencing.

"Pursuant to case 10098, the defendant, Marco Juarez, has been found guilty on one count of grand theft as well as one count of aggravated assault without a deadly weapon. The defendant has violated his previous probation sentence for which he will be tried at a later date. For these crimes, the defendant will serve a mandatory sentence of 151 months of imprisonment in our county's penitentiary. Upon release from imprisonment, the defendant shall be placed on supervised release for a term of 60 months."

As the implications of the judge's decision sink in, Gladys begins to sob. Gabi, the family's emotional anchor, wraps her arm around her mother to console her while her father breaks from his statuesque position, stands up, and strides out of the courtroom. The judge resumes his proceedings, but the remaining female family members are too distraught to listen or comprehend his words. At last, the bailiff forces Marco to stand up in his hand and foot chains and shuffles him out of the court room. As he's escorted away, he glances over at his mom and sister, who watch the entire scene with profound sadness. Marco, however, shows no trace of remorse: he simply turns his head away and follows the bailiff through a door that leads to the prisoner waiting area.

Stunned by what has just transpired, Gladys and Gabi take a moment to muster the strength to rise from their seats and leave the court room. A weeping Gladys pushes the door open with a fist clenched around a soggy tissue.

Meanwhile, Joel paces back and forth in the hallway. In the aftermath of his son's sentencing, his anger has transformed into misplaced guilt, complete with self-flagellation, shame, and angry self-talk. When he catches sight of his wife and daughter he barks, "What did I do wrong? I gave him everything but still it wasn't enough." Her face glistening from constant weeping, Gladys looks at him with a puzzled expression. Why the sudden shift from his previous attitude of anger and resentment? It didn't make sense.

"What? How can you say that?"

"I failed him, Gladys! Our son is going to jail. No, to prison, and it's our fault! We should have --"

"But, I'm good," Gabi interrupts meekly. "I'm good, Dad. You raised me in the exact same home as Marco and I'm a good person. I'm not like him, I don't do drugs. I get good grades and don't steal from people." In a tone that grows increasingly confident, she continues, "You didn't do anything wrong or else I'd be like him too, right? Marco took everything from you and Mom, but me? I do nothing but stay in the background while you and Mom focus on Marco." As she thinks about how her brother's addiction has robbed her of her parents' attention and rendered her all but invisible, Gabi's tone transforms from confident to furious. "Marco is going to jail! He's going away for a long time but I'm still right here!"

Joel stares at his daughter, trying to comprehend her pleas. Unfortunately, his focus has been on Marco's issues for so long, he can't bring himself to acknowledge what she is trying to tell him. "Ack, I don't need any more stress from my kids today," he declares as he turns his back to her and makes his way to the exit.

The three of them don't say another word to each other. Overcome by parental guilt, Joel leads his wife and daughter through the massive parking lot with the help of his car key's panic button. Consumed by insurmountable sorrow, Gladys trails behind and wipes her tears with the back of her hand. Finally, still invisible to her parents, Gabi walks at her own slow pace behind both.

They find their car and pile in. Gabi reaches for her purse, which she'd stowed in the space under the seat in front of her and reaches for her phone.

10:24am Tweet by: @GabiGabberz94
"It's over. He won't be coming home for a while. :(Prayers for me and the fam. It didn't' even seem like he cared, at least, I don't think he did."

PART 4

"IT WAS the worst day of my life."

Marco sits in the recreational room straddling a plastic chair facing another inmate. A correctional officer stands about ten feet behind him, next to the doorway, with arms crossed as he stares at the two inmates who are engrossed in conversation. In the background, the TV is on, but the sound is muted.

"I stood there, still feeling dope-sick, while the judge asked me if I had anything I wanted to say before he sentenced me." Marco smiles, "The worst part was, the whole time I could feel my dad's eye's glued to the back of my head." The other prisoner lets out a small laugh and keeps listening.

"What was I supposed to say? I knew he was going to lock me up, no matter what clever words I tried to spew out. Nothing I said was going to make any difference in what he decided to do with me." Marco pauses to wipe his nose with his thumb and leans back a little on his seat, holding onto the back rest with his hands. "The judge rambles off my sentence and I barely heard a word he said. I wanted a hit of something, anything to stop the withdrawals so badly that my hand was shaking all over the place."

"Man, I know that feeling," the other prisoner remarks.

Marco continues, "When they stood me up to walk me out and bring me here, I looked back at my mom and sister sitting there hugging each other, just looking at me all helpless." Marco shakes his head, "What scares me the most about that moment when I think about it, was how little I even cared that they were upset." He pauses as if to relive it again in his head. "I just looked at them. They were both crying but all I could think about was getting out of that room."

"Five minutes, gentlemen," the correctional officer bellows after noticing the time on the clock mounted on the wall.

Marco stands up and pushes the chair he was straddling back under the nearby table where he found it. "Hardest part about being in here, for me, isn't being away from them either. In fact, they're probably better off without me. No, the hardest part of being here is that I have to sit here, day after day, stone-cold sober. At least if I was high, time would fly by fast, right?" Marco lets out a small laugh, signaling his agreement with himself. Then, his eyes widen, and his face becomes serious. "There's got to be a way for me to find something in this shithole."

He sighs and looks down at his shoes in despair. On the surface, to his fellow inmates, he tries to maintain an image that being in prison hardly affects him, but the truth is, he is suffering tremendous emotional pain. He stopped using drugs to "pass the time" years ago; he now wants drugs in prison because he doesn't want to feel the way he feels about himself anymore. He needs them to escape the hard truth about what he's done to himself and his family. In fact, the prospect of getting high and relieving his mental torment overrules the fact that his own behaviors surrounding his drug use landed him in prison to begin with.

The inmates walk out of the recreational room together,

towards their cells. Once outside of earshot of any guard, Marco's companion leans in to him and whispers, "I might know a way to help you find what you're looking for in here."

His interest piqued, Marco lifts his head and looks into the eyes of his fellow prisoner with an eager expression on his face.

"You do?" he whispers.

PART 5

THE NEXT MORNING in the cafeteria, Marco sits at a corner table by himself eating his breakfast when he feels someone's hand hit him in the middle of his back. "I was told you were looking for something."

He looks over his shoulder to see an extraordinarily tall man standing behind him. Aside from his remarkable height, the man's tattoos – plastered across his face, the top of his head, and both of his arms – command attention. A shocked Marco offers a blank stare for a moment, trying to maintain a "poker face," so as not to belie his feelings. "What?" he replies, breaking the awkward silence.

"I heard you were looking for what I got. True or nah?"

It takes Marco a few seconds to realize what this ink-covered giant is offering him. He thinks back to his conversation in the recreational room the previous evening and how he felt at the time. After a night's rest, he feels a little better and decides he doesn't want to get involved with whatever this man is offering. After all, everything in prison comes with a steep price; at this moment, he isn't willing to pay it.

"No, man. I'm good," Marco replies as he turns back around

to finish his breakfast. For what feels like an eternity, the man continues to stand right behind him; Marco can feel his ominous presence. A palpable chill electrifies his spine, forcing him to straighten up in his seat. With all the effort he can muster, he stares forward into space while he waits for him to walk away.

"I don't come asking twice, so if you change your mind, you better come find me," the man announces. He moves away from Marco in a slow, careful pace while he scans the room for any perceived threats his paranoid mind can conjure. It's the mannerism only someone who's been in prison a long time would understand and recognize.

Marco lets out a big exhale and shakes his head. "Jesus, fu... God," he sighs. Just as he picks his spork back up, the deafening noise of a siren pierces the silence of the cafeteria. Marco drops his utensil, crouches his head down, and puts his hands over his ears. Suddenly, a large group of correctional officers storm in and shout out orders for everyone to return to their cells for a headcount. All prisoners, including Marco, obey the command, though they complain to each other about their breakfast being "pointlessly" interrupted as they file out.

Random headcounts are a normal part of the day-to-day scene in this prison, so no one is alarmed or shocked. It's the guards' way of keeping the prisoners on their toes and preventing them from thinking they have figured out the prison staff's routines. This time, however, all they have managed to do is agitate and annoy the inmates with the overwhelming blare of the siren that reverberates throughout the prison until they reach their assigned cells.

Marco sits down on his bed in his two-person cell alone. His cellmate was released just three days prior, so until they replace him, he is enjoying his privacy. He rotates his body and lays on his bed face-up, resting his head on the makeshift pillow he created using his extra uniforms. A week into his stay, some guards took his real pillow and have yet to replace it. They claimed it was for Marco's protection because his former violent cellmate tended to steal pillows in the middle of the night, but judging by their laughter, it was most likely a cruel prank on their newest charge.

He puts his hands under his head to support his neck a little better and waits for the guards to reach his cell and include him in the prisoner headcount so he can get on with his day. With nothing to pass the time, Marco's mind wanders back to what transpired in the cafeteria with the large, tattooed man. Anyone who's been inside the mind of an addict knows that time to think and an open window to score can be a deadly combination.

PART 6

FROM THE SECOND story of the prison, the inmates can hear the guards talking as they make their way from cell to cell. "I can't believe I actually turned down getting high earlier," Marco says out loud to himself. "Since when do I do something like that?" He turns to lay on his side and puts his elbow under his head. "How would I even pay for it, if I did take him up on his offer?"

His mind begins to run wild envisioning multiple ways the prison dealer might accept payment. Suddenly, the color drains out of his face as he remembers all the jokes that he and his prison friends used to make about prison buddies named "Bubba," and what they'd do to you if they got you alone. His complexion becomes as gray as the prison décor in his cell. Coming to his senses, he declares, "No, no. I don't think that's what he wanted." He sighs with relief while he continues to think about what he could use as a form of payment, if he wanted to take the dealer up on his offer. "Oh...commissary! I'd give them money from my commissary," he concludes.

He faces his next mental hurdle the moment he realizes he doesn't have any money on his commissary. He then flips through a cerebral rolodex of who he could call to transfer money into his account once this head-count ordeal is over. Marco recalls every person he's spent time with recently before coming to prison but eliminates them one-by-one as he realizes none of them are sober enough to cough up any dough. And since all his high-school friends who have either moved on to college or found gainful employment no longer speak to him, they're out.

"I guess I'd have to call my parents," he figures, with a bewildered look on his face. "But how would I ever get them to agree to give me money?" Marco scans the room and notices an empty package of prison-issued potato chips his old cellmate left in the trash can. "Food," he exclaims loud enough for the prisoner in the next cell to hear.

"You goin' to have to wait until lunch, bruh. They ain't lettin' us go back for our breakfast."

"Yeah, thanks," Marco yells back.

In his mind, he devises a plan to plead with his mother and father to put money on his account. He's going to tell them that prison food is terrible, and he needs money to buy snacks out of the commissary to hold him over in-between meals. "There's no way they'll tell me no. Mom can never let me go hungry."

That's the insidiousness of addiction. Without even realizing it, Marco has officially made the decision to get high in prison and hatched a plan to make it happen. With a fresh plot in his head and a growing urge to use, he lays on the bed and waits for the guard. When the guard walks up, sees him, clicks his counter, and moves past the cell Marco calls out, "Hey, Officer, what time do phone privileges start?"

PART 7

"Babe, how am I going to cheat on you? I'm locked up! There ain't no girls in here!" The next in line for the phone, Marco laughs out loud – along with the other prisoners – over the one-sided conversation they are overhearing between an inmate and his girlfriend. "Babe...Babe...listen to me. Don't hang up. No, don't han..." The man turns around to face the others in line with a baffled look on his face. "She hung up on me," he announces, shaking his head as he replaces the receiver.

With sweaty palms, Marco picks it up and dials his parents' home number. As the phone starts to ring, a feeling of dread washes over him, followed by the flash of a stock-ticker scrolling through his mind, screaming, "I shouldn't be doing this."

Ring.

His eyes blink closed, and his head shakes away his doubts about what he's about to do. It's an ability only a seasoned addict acquires, in which they can turn off morality like a subconscious light switch at the command of a sinister biblical creature that possesses them.

Ring.

His stomach begins to flip-flop, causing him to squirm in his shoes. Suddenly, someone picks up on the other line. An automated voice says, "Please state your name."

"Marco."

The startling, ear-piercing noise of someone on the other end pushing a button to accept the call forces him to pull the receiver away from his ear a little.

"Marco? Marco? Are you there? Are you okay? What's wrong?"

"Ma, I'm fine. I'm just calling to check in with you."

"Why haven't you called me yet? It's been weeks and we haven't heard from you! Where have you been?"

"Ma, I only have a couple minutes. There's a line of guys behind me." Attempting to make small talk he asks, "How's Dad? Gabi?"

Gladys sighs into the phone. "They miss you. We all do. Are you doing okay?"

"Yeah, I'm fine, Ma. It's freezing in here, it smells bad, and the people aren't what I would call friendly but I'm okay." During the silent pause that follows, Marco searches for an opening to accomplish his money-grab mission. Gladys, feeling like she hardly knows the boy she's speaking to, resorts to her maternal instinct.

"Are you eating enough?"

Marco's eyes light up like someone who just won the grand prize on a daytime television game show. Finally, the opening he was looking for! He plays to his mother's perceived weaknesses by dramatizing, "Actually, Ma, now that you ask, no, I'm not. The food is like slop in here. It's exactly like you see in movies. It's barely edible and, what I can eat, runs right through me."

"What? Put a guard on the phone. I'm going to talk to him and tell him what you like. You have to eat, or you'll never get better."

"It doesn't work like that, Mom. The guards don't care."

Then, to seal the deal he continues, "The only thing you can do to help me out is put money on my commissary account. Here, I'll give you my account number and then you just have to call the main jail line and ask for financial services. My account number is 9987 --"

Glady cuts him off, "Oh," she sighs again. "Honey, I can't put money on your account," she informs him in a matter-of-fact tone.

"Ma, I've only got like one minute left on the phone. Let me give you the account number!"

Unmoved by her son's pleas, Gladys explains, "Scott says we can't give you any money."

"Who the hell is Scott?" Marco demands, becoming more enraged by the second.

"Scott is the therapist your father and I have been seeing. He's helping us with our codependency. He said we can only give you love and verbal support, but no money."

"You're going to listen to him and let me starve?" Marco retorts indignantly as he takes one last, manipulative shot. "Scott? Are you kidding? Tell Scott he can go fu –"

"Your call has ended," reports an automated, female voice, followed by an obnoxious dial tone. Marco slams the receiver down and rubs his face with his hand. He starts to walk away, then turns to pound the wall with his fist in frustration as he releases a primal grunt.

"Inmate! Back away from the phones and go back to your cell!" a nearby officer yells as he points at him. Through gritted teeth, Marco looks at the person next in line and announces, "It's all yours." He walks back to his cell with a bright red face and throbbing fist. On the way, he spots the enormous tattooed man towering over everyone else as he stands near a group of people playing cards. Marco changes direction and approaches him with such ferocity that even the big guy backs up a few steps. "I changed my mind. I don't got money; what can I do to get some?" he asks, wild-eyed.

To Marco's surprise, the man grabs him by the shirt and shoves his back into a nearby wall with enough force to make him wince from the pain. "You never say that shit out in the open like that again!" He puts a finger in Marco's face, "Next time...I'll kill you."

As he walks away, Marco pleads in desperation, "C'mon, man. I'm sorry! Hey, I'm sorry, you hear? Look, I'm just trying to get something to chill me out. What do I have to do? C'mon, bro! You told me to come find you if I changed my mind, so I did that."

With his back to Marco, the giant turns his head around slightly and orders, "Just shut the fuck up...and follow me." Marco waves his hands in the air to signify, "It's all good, man," and obliges. He follows his lead to a far corner of the prison's common area.

The dealer walks into his cell and stops in front of the farthest wall. Exercising caution, Marco stands in the doorway. "Come in here," the colossus commands. Marco flashes back to the "Bubba" jokes he and his friends used to make. "Um, I'm okay right here," he replies meekly.

"I'm not yelling across the damn cell, come in here." With dead eyes, he glares at Marco while he waits for him to obey the order. Marco takes a loud gulp, walks into the cell and asks, "What's your name?"

"They call me Small Rick," he answers with obvious pride.

"Of, course they do." Marco notices that Small Rick is not amused by his sarcasm, so he continues. "What can I do to score some dope? I told you I don't have money."

"Yeah, I heard you, but there are other ways to make this work." Marco begins to sweat. He picks at his thumb with his pointer finger to relieve his frazzled nerves. "Oh, yeah?" he asks.

"Here's the deal: I get out in two days and I'm going to need some cash once I do."

"Oh, I can call my dad to see if he knows anyone who's hiring?" Marco naively suggests.

"Man, no one's hiring me! Look at me!" Marco agrees with his eyes but doesn't dare say a word. Rick continues, "I need a house to hit in the area where I can steal some shit to sell. What I need from you is your address and your family's schedule so I can hit the house when they're not home. I'll be in and out without even seeing any of them." He crosses his arms and stands up straighter, "You do that, and I'll get you hooked up."

Flabbergasted, Marco retorts, "What? No way, man. I'm not giving you my parents' address."

"Well, then you're shit out of luck. No one's giving you shit without any money. This is your only chance to get something going in here."

Marco's eyebrows curl together in confusion. When he thinks back to the call he just had with his mother, his blood begins to boil again. As he considers Rick's offer, he squints so hard his irises are barely visible. "If you do this, no one gets hurt. I need to know that with a thousand percent certainty."

"I said I want to go in when no one's home. How am I going to hurt someone when no one is there?"

Marco rubs his chin, runs his hand through his hair and turns around to think. As he stares out into the center of the prison where the inmates are playing cards on metal tables, he notices the miserable expressions on their faces. He looks around at the depressing gray walls before fixing his gaze on his tiny cell across the way. A chilling wave of reality overpowers any delusions he had about the hopelessness of his situation. It's a bleak realization Marco's mind cannot cope with, and because he knows no other way to manage his emotions, he makes an ominous decision.

"Alright, I'll do it. But, seriously, no one gets hurt. You're in and out, okay?"

"Yeah, sure. Whatever you say."

Marco ignores his first reaction of worry and skepticism, choosing instead to write down his family's address on a piece of paper with a small pencil one would find at a mini-golf course. He places it in Small Rick's hand and looks up at him for further instruction.

"Today's Tuesday. By Sunday, Big G will find you and give you your piece."

"Let me guess, Big G is a tiny guy?"

"What? No, why would you say that?"

Marco stares into the hollow eyes of the devil with whom he just made a deal, then slowly turns around and makes his way out of the cell. He brings his fingers to his mouth and takes a few nervous bites at the skin around his nails. Filled with buyer's remorse, he shakes his head as he walks across the center of the prison and wonders, "What the hell did I just do?"

PART 8

THE WEEK PASSES and Sunday finally rolls around. During this time, Marco has hardly left his cell, except to eat breakfast and check the clock hanging on the wall in the recreational room, which seemed to mock his impatience. Daily, he'd trek to and from the recreational room at least a dozen times, only to look at the clock, then make a sharp turn on his heels to return to his cell.

Pacing back and forth in his tiny cell is all he can do to pass the time; he can't focus on anything but the delivery he's supposed to have coming to him. "Where the hell *is* he?" he mutters to himself under his breath.

As he paces, he shakes his head as if he knows something has gone terribly wrong and his drugs won't be delivered to him as promised. "He should have found me by now. He told me to wait right here. What could this guy possibly be doing? He's not coming, I know it. This whole thing was stupid, and to make it all worse, I gave my parents' address to a known criminal."

Marco releases a primal groan, much like a wounded animal. "They better be okay," he declares – as if he has any control over the situation he set in motion. He stops pacing and throws his hands up in the air before walking out of his cell towards the recreational room again.

"8:33 p.m.," he whispers to himself. "What the hell is going on!?" For a moment, he stands in the recreational room questioning whether he should go looking for the man named "Big G." After giving it some thought, he decides to return to his cell to wait it out – just as he'd done the last few times he got the bright idea of searching for Big G.

Back at his cell, Marco resumes pacing back and forth before trying something new. He transitions to a seated position on the edge of his bed, leaning forward with his elbows resting on his knees. As is his habit when anxiously awaiting the arrival of his drugs, he bites his nails and cuticles. However, his right leg bounces with so much violence that when it bumps into his elbow, it causes his already bloodied fingers to miss his mouth.

"Oh my God, I'm a damn wreck right now," he laughs. In the next moment, levity gives way to worry, and he breathes a heavy sigh. "I told them the exact times they are usually out of the house, so they should be fine," he assures himself. "Maybe they changed their mind and didn't even hit the house."

Marco's eyes dart around the room as panicked thoughts reverberate through his brain. "Wait, he didn't say what day he was going. What if he went on Saturday instead of during the week? I gave them their Monday through Friday schedule during work and school hours. Oh, God, what have I done?" He jumps up and paces back and forth in his cell again.

"Okay, it's fine. They might have not gone at all. It's a huge risk for someone to take right out of prison; maybe he changed his mind and didn't go through with it." With that, Marco stops pacing again to peek out of his cell. "Where the hell is this guy?" Just as he finishes questioning the whereabouts of his delivery man, he notices another inmate – whom he can only assume is "Big G" – walking towards him, making eye contact. Although his body is frozen, Marco's feet somehow move enough to carry him to the back of his cell, his stomach churning.

As the inmate approaches and places a hand into his pocket, he grins from ear-to-ear, an expression Marco finds especially jarring. The smirk remains on his face when he steps inside. "You Marco?"

"Yeah."

The inmate reaches into his pocket, produces a small bag filled with a white-ish powder, and tosses it to Marco, who notices the bag's content has an unmistakable brown tint. He catches it with his right hand and slowly opens his fist to gaze at the heroin he's been waiting for all day. Then, for a fleeting moment, he appears less concerned with his heroin delivery and inquires with misty eyes, "So, he did it? He went to the address I gave him?"

"I wouldn't be here if he didn't." The inmate then reaches back into his pocket and grabs another small bag filled with a similar substance. He throws it at Marco with the announcement, "He said you earned two bags this time, too." Since he was still fixated on the first bag, the second bag hits Marco in the chest and falls to the floor. Confused, he looks up and asks, "Wait...what's that for? Why two bags?"

The haunting grin reappears on the inmate's face. "Rick said you gave him a bonus." He begins to back out of the cell as his grin evolves into a full-blown smile, revealing a mouthful of corroded teeth. "You've been holding out on us, bro! Rick found that baby sister of yours and told us she looked damn good!"

PART 9

THE COLOR DRAINS out of Marco's face. Left alone, he breathes hard with his mouth open, trying to comprehend what he just heard. As he looks down at what he holds in his hand, panic sets in. He drops the bag on the floor, where it lands next to the bonus bag Big G had thrown at him a second ago. Feeling his legs go wobbly, he backs into the wall and slides down into a crouched position.

A pounding wave of emotional terror overtakes him as he begins to sob with his head between his legs. In the next moment, he looks up through the ceiling with a tear-stained face for a showdown with God. "Why did you make me like this, huh?!" he screams. "I was a good kid! I didn't do anything to hurt anyone. I listened to my parents, my grandparents, and my teachers, so why am I this way? When did you decide it was a good time to change me into...this?!"

By now, his eyes are bloodshot, and his face soaked with tears as he leans his body forward onto all fours. He crawls towards the two bags of heroin, picks them up and falls back into his seated position against the wall. "All of this for this shit," he opens his hand and thrusts it towards the ceiling, as if trying to show God what he's holding. "Just tell me, why?! Huh, why?! Why am I like this?" Wracked by relentless sobs, he makes a fist and squeezes the two bags of heroin together. With his gaze on the ground, he slouches further down, all the life energy dissipating from his broken body.

"I'm so sorry, Mom. Dad, I'm sorry." He opens his drenched eyes wide and knits his brows together, thinking of his innocent baby sister. "Gabi, oh, Gabi. What have I done?" Marco weeps in solitude in the corner of his cold prison cell. A prisoner in more ways than one, he is overtaken by a grave despair only few can fathom. Slowly, he lifts his head from between his legs and wipes his face on his sleeve, directing his eyes to the ceiling once more.

"I love my family. I'm sorry, God, but please let them be okay. I know I've asked you to get me out of every horrible situation I've put myself in, but all those prayers were bullshit. This one, though, this one I mean with all my heart." He closes his eyes and whispers, "Please, I'm begging you."

Nearly cried out, Marco slinks back down. His breathing remains deep and shaky as his fingers remember what they are gripping and roll the bags of heroin against his palm. He turns his fist over to look at the drugs again. In an instant, a shift occurs: he's hypnotized and seduced by what's lying in his grasp. With fluttering eyelids and staccato breaths, he frowns his lips in disgust.

"God doesn't listen to people like me," he remarks as he throws one of the baggies onto the ground, still gripping the other. A possessed man, Marco stands up, wipes the remaining tears on his dry sleeve, and pours a small portion of the full bag onto the countertop in his cell. In the blink of an eye remorse, guilt, and shame fall victim to the primordial skewed reasoning of an addicted mind. Enamored by the powerful sedative before him, Marco leans forward and places his pointer finger over one nostril, fully prepared to blow away another line of morality he's yet to blur.

"I love my family. I really do and I'm so sorry for everything I've put them through," he tells himself as he comes face-to-face with a readied – if somewhat messy – line of heroin. He takes a deep breath in through his open nostril, snorting the drug off the counter. For a moment, his eyes roll towards the back of his skull. Relief, though fleeting, calms his pulsating heart. Marco's eyes gaze at the beguiling devil sprawled out and sunbathing across his prison-issue countertop with all the passion and romance of a lover.

Raising an eyebrow, he professes, "But, I love you, more."

STORY THREE

PART 1

"I CAN'T CLOSE my eyes without that moment replaying over again in my mind."

Even with close to 30 people in attendance, you could've heard a pin drop – save for the sound of a coffee pot percolating on a table along the wall. Displayed on a platter right next to it are freshly baked chocolate-chip cookies, courtesy of one of the group members.

Tracy continues, "It's been four months since Brittany's overdose. Four months since she left her earthly body." With a forced smile, she looks at the crowd and wipes a tear from under her eye with her thumb. "It's just, it still doesn't feel real, you know? I'm still waiting for her walk in through the front door and throw her purse on the coffee table like she always did." She pauses for a moment to take a deep breath as a few attendees shift in their seats, creating a temporary, voluminous sound of busyness. Tracy exhales and forces another smile at a woman she recognizes in the front row.

"You can do this," the woman encourages her.

"I know. I can do this." Tracy inhales and exhales deeply one more time. "You know, as crazy as this sounds, I swear Brittany is still with me. It's like I can feel her in the room with me or some-thing. Whenever a song plays on the radio that the two of us listened to together, I feel like it's her trying to say something to me."

Some people nod in understanding, having experienced similar thoughts or feelings in the aftermath of the loss of their loved one. "Four months sounds like a long time, but I feel like I'm still living in the day I found her in her room with that needle in her arm." Tracy rubs the inside of her elbow as if she could feel it in her own arm. "I don't know how I'm supposed to feel at this point in my grief recovery. Sometimes, I feel guilty that I don't feel stronger sadness or anger but it's like I'm numb to it. Like my brain won't let me feel the full force of the loss because if I could, I'd go crazy. Maybe I already have." She squeaks out a short laugh and the rest of the group laughs with her. Then someone in the back of the room lets out a loud, "Mm-hm," in agreement.

Another woman who is seated in the row holding a notepad in her hand, asks, "Tracy, sweetie, are you eating? Are you sleeping?"

"Um, I'm trying. I've been keeping track of my sleep in a journal next to my bed. I'm getting better. This past Monday I got five hours; I think I woke up a couple times but at least I stayed in bed that whole time. As far as eating goes, I know I need to try harder. It's just so hard. I feel like I'm choking or can't swallow the food. Like my body, metaphorically, can't swallow what happened." The woman scribbles something down, then looks back up at Tracy. "You've come a long way, sweetie. Is there anything else you want to say to the group?"

Tracy thinks for a moment. She picks up her phone from the podium in front of her to look at the time, but unintentionally notices the date. "It's her birthday next week." Her face begins to scrunch up to fight off tears that come anyway. "She would have been twenty. My little girl." She looks down at the podium and pulls a tissue out of a strategically placed box. Before every meeting, the woman with the notepad places boxes of tissues throughout the room for the aid and comfort of attendees.

The group leader sets down her notepad and rises from her chair, "Thank you for that lovely share, Tracy," she compliments. The room erupts with applause as Tracy makes her way to her seat, half-waving to the group with a fist clenched around a tissue in a gesture of gratitude for their support.

"Well, that's it for tonight everyone. Every one of you said some truly powerful words this evening and I feel I speak for everyone when I say that a lot of healing went down during this last hour." The group nods in agreement. "I'll see all of you next week and, don't forget, wherever you are in the grieving process is exactly where you're at!"

In a simultaneous motion, each member stands and begins hugging the person to their left and right. Tracy and the man who had been sitting to her right make their way towards the front door to leave. "Wherever you are in the grieving process, is exactly where you're at," he mimics the group facilitator in a mocking tone. "What the fuck does that even mean?"

Tracy laughs politely and shakes her head from side to side. "I don't know what it means, really, but for some reason I find it comforting." The two exchange smiles once they reach the parking lot, then go their separate ways towards their cars.

As she slips into the driver's seat, Tracy puts her phone in the cupholder and places her hand on the gearshift to reverse out of her parking spot. In the next instant, she pulls her hand back to grab her phone, open her to-do list, and make an entry:

Pick up a cake and candles for Brittany's B-day next week.

PART 2

THE TRUNK SLAMS down as Tracy balances a string of grocery bags slung onto one arm and carries an ice-cream cake in the other. Frosted, cursive writing on the cake reads "Happy Birthday, Brittany." She makes her way to the front door with the house keys dangling from her hand and unlocks it. Once inside, she throws the heavy bags onto the counter with a big groan as two cats scurry into the kitchen to greet her.

"Hi, little boys," she acknowledges them with excitement, still holding the cake in her hand. "Look what I got for Brittany's birthday," showcasing the cake to her cats.

She opens the freezer door and puts the cake on an empty shelf. Before she closes the freezer, she stares at her daughter's name on the cake and places her hand gently on top of the box, as if softly petting her Brittany's head. She breathes deeply in through her nose and out through her mouth, then swallows hard to stop herself from crying. Then, she pulls her hand away and closes the freezer door, returning her attention to her cats.

"What did you guys do all day without me? Did you miss Mommy?" In typical feline fashion, one of them weaves between her legs, creating a figure eight-like shape, while the other walks out of the room, uninterested.

The quiet house is too big for one person to live in. Laden with pictures of Tracy and Brittany, it feels as if it's become a memorial to better times gone by. Tracy notices a flashing light on the old answering machine Brittany always made fun of her for using. The two of them often laughed about Tracy's insistence on keeping a land-line phone. "What if our cell phones stop working? Then who will be the one laughing," Tracy used to joke back, half-serious.

She walks over to the answering machine and hits the play button to listen to her messages. "Hey, Tracy. It's Maggie. Just calling to check on you and see if --" Tracy punches the "next" button on the machine, cutting off the message mid-sentence.

"Tracy, hey, it's me. I've called five times now and I'm starting to worr --"

Next.

"Tracy. Are you home? Pick up the phone. Tracy? Alright, I guess you're not there so call me whe --"

Next.

"Hi, Tracy, Dr. Negin here. You didn't show for yesterday's appointment so I wanted to call to make sure I can still expect you next week." A nervous Tracy starts to chew on her finger but continues to listen as Dr. Negin's message continues, "Don't forget to bring something of Brittany's with you to our next session. Ideally it would be something personal to her. You mentioned she kept a journal throughout her last time in treatment; that would be perfect since it contains her most recent thoughts. Okay, if I don't hear back, I'll just assume that I'll be seeing you next week. Bye-bye."

Tracy pivots her head to look towards Brittany's closed door at the end of the hallway as she continues to gnaw on the skin around her thumbnail. "End of messages," the answering machine reports, disrupting the silence in the room. With her eyes fixated on Brittany's door, Tracy takes a step towards the hallway.

"I can do this," she says confidently. She moves in the direction of the bedroom, placing one foot in front of the other as if trying to make as little noise as possible. With a hand outstretched to the doorknob, Tracy inches closer, but the closer she gets, the slower she moves. When she arrives within a couple of feet of the doorway, she pauses to take a few deep breaths. "It's just an empty bedroom filled with stuff. I can open that door and walk in and I'll be totally fine."

Now inches away from the doorknob, she stretches her hand out further until – zap! A spine-tingling shiver shoots up her spine and forces the hairs on her arms to stand straight up in the air. Tracy's hand recoils from the object as if it's a scorching flame. In a flash, she turns and rushes back to the hallway to get as far away as she can from the closed door of her deceased daughter's bedroom. When she makes it back to where her journey began, she looks back at the same doorway she walked through four months ago when she discovered her only child's lifeless body sprawled across her bed with a needle sticking out of her arm. Haunted by the memory, Tracy puts her thumb in her mouth and resumes gnawing at her skin.

"Tomorrow. Tomorrow, I'll go in there." She exhales a deep sigh of relief. "Yes, tomorrow, not today. Today is not the day."

PART 3

A LOUD CRASHING noise jars Tracy out of her half-slumber. She glances at the clock next to her bed which reads, "3:33 a.m." She rubs her eyes and notices the intense sound of silence that fills her empty home. Since losing Brittany, Tracy and her therapist consider a couple hours of rest a "good night." It takes Tracy a moment to determine that the noise was simply her exhausted mind playing tricks on her. After a few seconds of continuous silence, she lays her head back down on her pillow, satisfied with the idea that what she heard was a product of her imagination. Within a few minutes, her eyelids become heavy and start to close -- only to open wide in reaction to another crashing noise.

"That was definitely in the house," a panicked Tracy says out loud. As she jumps out of bed, she startles her two slumbering cats, who'd been curled up by her feet, causing them to scatter out of the room. She drops to her knees and reaches under her bed to pull out the baseball bat she hides there for protection. With a tight grip around it, Tracy tiptoes towards her bedroom door, on high alert.

"Hello?" she whispers in a loud voice.

Silence.

"Is somebody there?" she repeats louder, her fists still clenched around the wooden bat.

Silence.

With slow, calculating steps, she makes her way into the living room and notices that everything remains undisturbed. Feeling some relief, Tracy loosens her grip on her self-defense weapon and walks over to the front door to confirmed it's still locked. It is.

"I'm losing my mind," she chuckles, shaking her head at her own behavior. But as she returns to her bedroom directly across the hallway from Brittany's, she hears another startling crash and realizes it's coming from Brittany's room. Tracy's heart sinks into her stomach; instinctively, she moves to cover her dropped jaw with her hand.

"Oh my God. Brittany!" Tracy screams as she runs towards her deceased daughter's door. "Brittany, is that you?!" She barrels into the room as if she never struggled to open the door before. "Brit..." her voice begins to fade off "...tany." To her obvious disappointment, the sight that awaits her is not the miracle of her resurrected child, but a bookcase with three collapsed shelves. Books, pictures, and papers are scattered throughout the floor. Tracy crouches down to get a better look at the mess.

Then she's hit by a powerful realization: for the first time in four months, she has entered Brittany's room. With eyes widening, she stands up as a strange sense of familiarity overtakes her. Looking around the room, she acknowledges, "It's exactly how she left it." Tracy's eyes begin to well with tears.

In a pseudo-state of shock, she gingerly sits on the bed and reaches back to grab one of Brittany's old pillows. She holds it close to her chest and nestles her face into it, hoping to get a whiff of the slightest trace of her daughter's sweet-smelling shampoo in its fibers. Taking a deep inhale, Tracy closes her damp eyes. With no scent in that spot, she moves the pillow around and sniffs in desperation for any lingering aromas. She finds a promising area she believes could carry her daughter's familiar scent and breathes in with everything she's got to ignite a clear image of her daughter in her mind – if only for a fleeting moment.

Tracy closes her eyes while she inhales through her nose, but in the next second, the flash of another image takes her breath away. In the theater of her mind, she returns to the moment of that horrific discovery and sees her daughter's cold, dead body lying on the bed – the same one she is sitting on right now. Shocked by the flashback, she springs up, gasping for air. Horrified, Tracy throws the pillows back onto the bed and runs to the door to make a quick escape. But just as she reaches the doorway, the voice of her therapist reverberates in her head:

"Don't forget to bring something of Brittany's with you to our next session. Ideally it would be something personal to her."

Tracy scans the pile of books on the floor and spots a black-and-white spotted journal with the inscription, "2018" and the name of her last treatment center written on it in marker. She scurries over as fast as she can, grabs the journal, and then tears out of the room, slamming the door behind her. The sound of her footsteps on the hardwood floor of the hallway echoes throughout the vacant home.

PART 4

"I RAN IN THERE, yelling her name like some psychopath who believed my dead daughter was really alive and decided to come home," Tracy recounts to her therapist, Dr. Negin. "I buried her, I watched her casket get lowered into the ground, yet it still doesn't feel completely real."

Dr. Negin nods with sympathetic attention, then responds, "Do you remember discussing the stages of grief?" Tracy leans back in her chair and shakes her head in agreement. Dr. Negin continues, "Good, then you'll remember the first stage of grief is shock and denial. What it sounds like you're telling me is that you're still experiencing some denial, even if it is on a subconscious level. Would that be an accurate statement to make?"

"It's been four months! And what I'm hearing you tell me is that I'm still only on the first stage! How's that for an accurate statement, doc?" Tracy crosses her arms, leans forward and raises her eyebrows in anticipation of an answer from her therapist.

Dr. Negin takes off his glasses and places his notepad and pen on the small end-table next to his chair. Leaning forward to match Tracy's body language, he explains, "Try not to think of it as being at the beginning of your grieving process. The stages of grief are simply a rough guideline for the progression you may experience when grieving the loss of a loved one. They don't always go in order; they sometimes flip-flop and sometimes they blur together." He pauses to offer her a reassuring smile, "You're doing everything you should be doing. There is no right and wrong way to feel right now."

Tracy slumps backwards into her chair and throws her hands in the air as her eyes begin to well again, "I just feel like I'm losing my mind."

Dr. Negin remains silent in the hope that his patient will continue. After a moment, Tracy adds, "I know you're right, but I just feel...I feel...lost. Completely confused all the time, sad...a lot. There are times where I catch myself talking to her like she's still with me, but the weird part is, I'm talking to the old Brittany. The sweet, innocent child version of her before she became corrupted by drugs." She grabs a tissue from the box off the coffee table and wipes her eyes. "That even makes me feel guilty, like I'm forgetting the last years of her life and just pretending she's still my sweet, little angel."

"It's up to you how you want to remember your daughter. Like I've said to you before, there is no right or wrong way to go through this," Dr. Negin explains.

"That shit – oh, sorry," Tracy apologizes, covering her mouth with her hand. In response, Dr. Negin offers a big grin. "It's okay, Tracy, I think I've heard that word a time or two. You were saying?"

"That stuff," she counters with a cheeky smile. "It destroyed her. I'd watch her lose weight, stop washing her hair, notice her skin turning gray...but then she'd go into treatment for a month and come back out looking like my daughter again, only to relapse and start the cycle all over."

"Cunning, baffling, powerful," Dr. Negin reminds her in a

matter-of-fact tone. "Addiction can have such an unrelenting pull on a person."

"Ugh, yes, and her attitude when she was using; forget it! I couldn't say anything to her without getting my head bit off!" She stops and stares at the floor.

"Are you okay, Tracy?" Dr. Negin asks.

"I'd just about do anything to hear her yell at me one more time."

The therapist decides to change the subject to direct Tracy's attention back to the present moment. "I see you brought Brittany's journal with you. Did you find anything in there you wanted to read in today's session?"

With an anxious look on her face, Tracy reaches for the journal. Using an old grocery store receipt, she'd bookmarked a page in preparation for this exercise. "Yeah, I found this. It's a letter she wrote to me, I guess. I feel like it's the most honest she's ever been with me, even though she never actually sent it."

Dr. Negin places his glasses back over his eyes, picks up his notepad and pen off the side-table and announces, "I'm ready when you are."

Tracy looks down at the words on the paper and takes a deep breath. "Okay, here it goes…"

PART 5

Hi Mom,

It's me, Brit, in the flesh coming to you live (well sort of) from day 49 of treatment. My therapist, Jackie, thought it would be a good idea for me to write you a letter since I'm having such a hard time describing how I feel in person. I'm still not sure if I'm going to send this to you or not but I guess that's not the point, anyway. She says writing this is not about me and you healing our relationship, since I can only do that over time by showing you I'm trying to get better, but it's about me "processing through my guilt and shame," over everything I've done to you over the years.

Honestly, I'd be surprised if you ever forgave me. Half the time I don't even know why you keep trying to help me. None of this comes as a shock to you at this point, but I've stolen from your purse, from the house, I've lied to you, made you worry night after night...all for what? So I can get high one more time? My life was, literally, Groundhog Day. I woke up every morning like I was on autopilot. My first thought was how was I going to get money from you, in one way or another, to get high for the day. And you, because of how much you love me, always opened the door for me at night to let me back in. Then I would wake up the next day and start the exact same process all over again.

So much has changed since middle school. We were so close, but I ruined that. Actually, my therapist told me I need to stop saying that "I" ruined my life, but that the drugs did. She has me doing these things called "positive affirmations" and tells me to look in the mirror five times a day and say, "I'm a good person with a bad disease." Ha ha! It's so cheesy but I guess it's supposed to help. So far, I just feel like a bad person with a bad disease but that's why I'm in therapy, right?

Anyway, I miss those days we had together. It's just been me and you for so long. When Dad died, I remember you telling me "We will always have each other, no matter what!" I don't even know how I remember that since I was only six when he passed away, but I do. I know things will never go back to how they were but I'm really hoping I can make things right again for us. You were my best friend and I just feel like I let you down so many times.

It's hard to explain but, in the moment, it was almost like someone hit an "off" switch in my brain and once that switch was flipped, I didn't care about you or anyone else anymore. Only one thing mattered, like I was a robot on a mission to get high. I had the occasional moment of clarity, here and there, usually really early in the morning when I was coming down, where I'd think about the effect I'm having on you. It was a fleeting worry that passed through my mind and I'd swear to myself that I was going to do something nice for you that day that would make up for it all. Then my anxiety would start to come back, my stomach would start to hurt, my skin would crawl, and I knew exactly what I needed to make me feel better. All my guilt for hurting you would just disappear, and it was like my body was going into survival mode. I was some sort of beast, or something, motivated purely by instinct instead of rational thoughts.

Regardless, none of that takes away what I've done to you. Whether I have a "disease" or not, doesn't mean it all wasn't my fault. I chose to get high that first time. I chose to relapse after my last three treatments. I like to think I tried but, really, I just tried by doing the bare minimum and when a craving hit me, I went with it because...I wanted to.

I'm sorry for everything, Mom. I really am. I'm sure that word has no meaning to you anymore, but I just have to say it again. I'm going to really try this time, I swear it! I don't want to do this to you again. I want to go to the mall with you and get our nails done together. I want my mom back and I'm sure you want me back too. At least, I hope you do. When I come home, things are going to be different, you'll see! You may not have the old me back, but you'll get Brittany 2.0, a new and improved version of me!

In the words of a very wise mother:

We will always have each other, no matter what!

Love You!

Brittany

PART 6

TRACY CLOSES her daughter's old journal and reaches for another tissue. When it becomes evident that one won't be enough to dry her soaking face, she reaches for another. Wiping her dripping nose, she looks at Dr. Negin for a clue as to what she is supposed to do next.

"I know that was difficult for you and I'm really proud of you for making it all the way through."

Tracy nods as she continues to dry her flowing tears. She dares not speak, for fear she will not be able to stop an impending breakdown. "I can see you're struggling to talk; why don't I tell you why I wanted you to read that to me." Dr. Negin removes his glasses and explains, "I was hoping that by reading something Brittany wrote in her own words, you would be able to form a new, final memory of her. I'm sure you, like me, could picture Brittany saying all those things to you in your mind. Her smile, her long hair, her little quirks only a mother would notice." Tracy stops crying for a moment as she focuses on what her therapist is telling her.

"I don't want the last image you have in your mind of your daughter to be the one from 'that day.' I wanted it to be a more positive one and I hope that by reading this, you're able to achieve that goal." Tracy wipes her face one last time and lets out a deep sigh. Still not ready to talk, she expresses herself with a small smile and a nod in his direction.

"Well, Tracy, time is up for today, but you did some excellent work in this session," Dr. Negin announces after glancing at his watch. Together, the two of them stand up and walk to the door. "I'll see you next week but, seriously, great job today."

"Dr. Negin? One last thing," Tracy says in a quiet voice. "I'm not ready to say goodbye to her, yet. I'm scared that if I'm working towards getting some type of closure, it's like I'm trying to forget about her or something."

Dr. Negin smiles and gently places his hand on her shoulder. "Brittany will always be with you; our job here is to help you find some peace with her passing. Working through grief is never about 'forgetting;' it's about moving past the pain caused by her leaving us so that you can begin to live a fulfilling life again."

Tracy forces another meek smile. Without uttering a word, she walks out his office and towards the elevator. While waiting alone in the hallway, she grips Brittany's journal in her hand. As her lip begins to quiver, she pulls the journal close to her face and kisses the front cover.

PART 7

THE FRONT DOOR of the house swings open and Tracy comes barreling in holding shopping bags on both arms. After tossing them on the couch, she enters the kitchen to greet her two cats. "Hello you little monsters! What did you do all day while Mommy was out shopping?"

The furry felines meow in response, as if attempting to communicate their excitement to see her. Tracy walks to the fridge to grab a bottle of water and notices the calendar pinned to the wall next to it. She looks at today's date and sees "Brittany's B-day" written in red ink. She opens the water bottle and takes a couple big gulps of pure, cold refreshment.

"We're going to have a cake for Brittany's birthday today," she announces to her kitties. Placing the bottle on the counter, Tracy opens the freezer, reaches in with both arms, and pulls out the ice-cream cake she'd placed in there a week ago.

"Happy Birthday, Brittany," she reads aloud from the cake, while the cats speak to her in alternating loud meows. Acknowledging them, Tracy exclaims, "I know; it's a big cake and it's all for us!" After placing it on the dining room table, she walks back into the kitchen to rummage through her drawers for candles.

She finds a mostly empty box and pulls out the last remaining one. "I guess one candle will have to do."

Tracy's energy seems positive as she moves with childish glee about the kitchen. Her therapist would say she is having a "good day," a phenomenon he hasn't witnessed in his patient in weeks. Despite her positive energy, however, the house is fully consumed with a palpable, eerie feeling of emptiness. But perhaps because it always feels cold and empty to her these days, Tracy does not even notice. The cats continue to cry as they crisscross around her feet.

She moves towards the frozen cake and pushes on the lone candle with all her strength to situate it in the center. Then she pulls a lighter from her pocket and lights the candle. Mesmerized by the flame, she pauses to stare at it for a moment until another loud meow from the cats forces her to refocus on the task at hand. She begins to sing quietly:

"Happy birthday to you. Happy birthday to you."

"Meow, meow," the cats cry out with increasing volume and urgency.

"Happy birthday to Brittany. Happy birthday to you."

Slowly, she moves her face closer until she is eye-level with the candle flame. For a moment, she stares at her daughter's name written in frosting, then smears it with her thumb and wipes it on her nose – something she used to do to make Brittany laugh when she was a young girl.

Before blowing out the candle, she smiles. A feeling of warmth consumes her, like a group hug from all her favorite people. "I love you, Brit," Tracy says with an expression of comfort on her face. The cats let out another voluminous meow as the candle on the cake flickers. A voice that only Tracy can hear whispers back, "I love you, more."

A MESSAGE FOR THOSE WHO ARE STRUGGLING

I am you and you are me. By that I mean, you are not alone. And it isn't just me who understands what you're going through; it's millions of others just like us who have stood face-to-face with addiction.

Our stories vary from person to person: we come from different parents, grew up in different towns, and have our own unique experiences, yet we share a common bond. Like a band of brothers and sisters, we relate to each other at a depth only a select few can understand, even if we've never met.

Why is that important? Like me, many others have overcome their demons – the same ones you are struggling with right now. It wasn't easy and it didn't happen overnight, but one day at a time, we dismantled our addiction. So long as you are breathing, there will always be hope that you can find the same type of recovery we have sought and found. The reality is that with effort, you can undo the damage you've done. Even though it may feel as if you've scurried too far down the rabbit hole, no one is incapable of making an epic comeback.

It all starts with a decision. Not just any decision, though. It isn't the casual "I'm not going to get high (or drunk) today," that we tell ourselves the morning after a particularly rough night. I'm talking about a decision borne of utter defeat, in which we extend a shaky hand and admit, "I can't do this anymore. I need help."

Many of us are too ashamed to make such a necessary and humbling choice because we believe it implies that we are weak-minded. But nothing could be further from the truth: the strongest (and smartest) people are the ones who recognize they cannot complete a task alone and employ the assistance of others to accomplish it.

I chose to waste as much time as I could by trying every tactic under the sun – except for placing myself at the mercy of others. It was a pride thing that not only wasted years of my life but endangered my life and livelihood. In my obstinance, I tried to go it alone, using my own recovery methods: working out at the gym, reading self-help books, watching motivational videos on YouTube, and utilizing the law of attraction to "will" my addiction away.

Although I tried talking to a therapist, I kept my substance abuse a secret from him, figuring if I worked on my other issues, maybe my body would suddenly stop craving drugs. Yeah...that didn't work out too well. In my attempt to "fake it until you make it," I pretended I didn't have an actual addiction yet somehow at the end of each night, my car transported me to my dealer's house, as if on autopilot.

Even after my family intervened and I went to a treatment center, I still tried to pretend like my problem wasn't as bad as it was. It took a group of my peers and a ferocious therapist to finally hold the mirror of reality up to my face. At that moment, I realized I had no idea what I was doing, and my life was in shambles. No one back home wanted anything to do with me, I had no money in my bank account, and my life lacked any semblance of direction. My bag of tricks was empty, and I needed guidance on what to do next because if I kept living my way, my family would have never come back into my life, nor would I have found serenity and peace-of-mind. I would have never saved my own life.

Saved my own life...the irony of that statement is that I saved my own life by letting others save me. Other people like me taught me how to function as a decent, productive, and civilized human being in the world, and to live a life without gratuitous substance abusing. They taught me the meaning of integrity, the practical application of honesty, and the reward that comes from working hard for something I want. I followed their suggestions and did as I was told because, after all, I had no idea what I was doing. My "I know everything" attitude was quickly replaced with "I don't know, can you show me?"

Today, I am living a life that exceeds my wildest dreams. I have everything I ever wanted and more. My family loves me and, more importantly, they trust me!

Please understand, I am not bragging. I am showing you what's possible once you surrender your way of doing things and trust those who understand what you're going through. You, too, can have what I have, in one way or another.

So, go get help. Call your parents, a loved one, a trusted friend, or a heavily researched treatment center. Explain your situation and ask for guidance. Ask for recommendations or if they know anyone who can help. Be open to suggestions, try everything, and don't give up until you find what works for you. You are worth it. Every single person is worth it.

I often hear the phrase "people can't change." From my first-hand experience I can tell you that is a crock of shit. I've changed. Hundreds of people I know, and millions I don't, have changed.

Regardless of your personal situation, recovery is possible. However, no one can do it for you: it's up to you to reach out and ask for help, then let those around you guide you to a better life. Like a sumptuous buffet, recovery is available for you, but you must get up and get it yourself. No one can or will serve it to you. You must do the work and follow through on others' recommendations. Will it be easy? Hell, no. It will be one of the hardest things you've ever done. Will it be worth it? Oh, hell yes.

So, get off your ass and make your move. The ball is in your court. Some temporary tears and pain now will reap you years of smiles and joy later.

Blake C.
Sober Date
December 31, 2012

A MESSAGE FOR THE FAMILIES

THE HARDEST THING for a person to do is watch a loved one slowly kill themselves while you stand by, unable to do anything about it. We want to shake them – as if doing so could unlock some hidden reserve of common sense stored away deep in their brain, just waiting to be released by a good, strong shove.

For the family, addiction can be frustrating, heart-wrenching, exhausting, and time-consuming. It can lead to bouts of anger followed by bouts of hysteria. It can leave you bed-ridden and paralyzed by insurmountable sadness and depression. I mention all of this to remind you of something very important:

Don't forget to take care of yourself.

It's way too easy to get caught up in the highs and lows of a family member with a substance use disorder. In fact, it's so easy that we end up forgetting that we have needs, too. We focus all our energy on devising plots to free our loved one from the scourge of addiction and leave nothing for ourselves. We ignore the rest of the family and give all our attention to the one who is addicted. We exhaust every ounce of money, time, and security in hopes that something we do will "cure" their affliction.

However, the hard truth is, we are incapable of making our loved ones better – just as we are not responsible for making them sick. I know that's a hard concept to accept, given that we've blamed ourselves for our loved one's addiction for so long, but it is crucial that you do accept this if you ever expect to be capable of living a "normal" life again.

Another cliché that comes to mind involves oxygen masks on an airplane. Before we take off for the friendly skies, the flight attendants review the safety precautions. They instruct us that in the unforeseen event of a loss of cabin pressure, we must place our own mask on first, before assisting the person next to us. After all, it would be rather difficult to put an oxygen mask on anyone else if you're unconscious in your seat.

Now, if you're thinking, "Blake, that's easier said than done," I hear you. But I never promised it would be easy. Much like an addict faces their unique challenges in finding recovery, you will face challenges in your recovery too…and yes, you too, are in recovery. It takes diligent work and much reliance on outside entities like therapists, friends, family, and support groups to move on from your experiences. You will have bad days – probably many of them in the beginning – but you will also have a growing number of good days once your new, healthy habits become repetitious.

You're not giving up on your loved one, by the way. You are taking care of yourself so that when the day comes that they reach out to you for help, you are strong enough to assist them. Your practice of self-care aids your mental stability so that you can accept the fact that your loved one may never recover. It enables you to embrace the reality of the moment and preserve your own sanity for the sake of the rest of your family, your friends, and your future.

Self-care is not selfish: even therapists see other therapists and take careful measures to avoid burn-out to better serve their patients. Go do something you enjoy. Talk to mental health professionals or find a support group. Begin the healing process you deserve. Like I've said, addiction is a family disease; recovery must take place for everyone affected by it. Now, go take a warm bubble bath. You've earned it.

SUBSTANCE ABUSE: A FATHER'S PERSPECTIVE

GARY COHEN

As a father of five adult children and brother to an elder and younger sibling, I have learned over my 63 years that substance abuse can strike any family at any time, even when there is no known direct genetic history. This often-devastating disease has many outcomes, but the only constant is that when it hits, its effect is not limited to the person afflicted. An entire unprepared family can be torn apart by the many unforeseen consequences of a brother or son suddenly turning into a different person from the one you thought you knew.

A wonderful and trusted son and brother can transform into a deceptive thief -- even a 28-year-old who never touched drugs or alcohol in his life and is about to become a doctor. He, too, can be wrenched away from his respectable career plans as a productive citizen to become a criminal and lifelong drug addict who ruins his life, his parents' dreams, and, ultimately, his long-term health.

In the case of my son, the author of this book, I witnessed the sudden downward spiral of a seemingly perfect young man into an unprecedented and convoluted web of lies I never thought possible.

I've since learned -- the hard way - that his behavior was classic for a drug abuser: denial after denial; blame on everyone else; and, once caught, remorse. He appears to go back to normal; then, in the blink of an eye, I receive a phone call about his arrest. Seeing your son in a drug court dock, handcuffed and looking like a stranger, is a shock you never recover from. That day, he was sentenced to a drug program -- a diversionary procedure -- and successfully completed the course. I breathed a sigh of relief, thinking it was over. It wasn't.

Within a brief period, he returned to his previous suspicious behavior, and my wife's pain pills began to disappear. Since I had learned lessons from my brother, I immediately confronted my son. After he confessed, I took him directly to a detox center, then arranged to send him out-of-state to a well-known drug and alcohol rehabilitation center for as long as it took. During this time, I forbade him to speak to his friends and family or come home for a visit before he was discharged. All my trust in him was gone...maybe forever. How *could* I trust him again after everything he'd put us through? His brothers and sisters – and especially his mother and I – were devastated. We all thought we lost him, like I had lost my brother.

Fortunately, we were wrong. Blake never made me so proud as when he finally came home. Not only was he committed to recovery, he made the decision to dedicate his life to helping others with this insidious disease. He never used again, never lied to us again and, eventually, gained back all the trust, confidence, and love he had lost. Believe me, it took a long time to completely restore this trust.

But restored it was!

Blake is one of the most remarkable success stories I've witnessed; however, there were many occasions when I truly doubted if this would be the case. Throughout the whole family's ordeal with addiction, we were angry, confused, and sick over what Blake had done and the uncertainty of what the future held for him and us. Along with his wonderful fiancé, we slowly let him back in. But don't be deceived: drug abusers are good con artists and it took far more than words to gain back our trust. It took years of proven deeds.

And in the end, our Blake returned to us -- the most generous, kind, and sensitive young man I know. He never stops working towards his goal of successfully helping every afflicted person he meets. He is a 24/7 friend to the hopeless and their families and has become an inspirational speaker all over the country. When there is a failure, he feels it personally and is profoundly affected. Yet he pushes even harder in the hope that he can make a difference, which he does every day. As his father, I couldn't be prouder. I love my son for the unique person he has become and the courage he displayed at the depths of despair. Unfortunately, this is not the case for countless other families.

If I can pass anything along to the loved ones of someone in the throes of addiction, it is this:

DO NOT CODDLE. DO NOT TRUST UNTIL TRUST IS EARNED. DO NOT BLAME YOURSELF AND DO NOT LET YOUR LOVED ONE BLAME YOU! DO NOT HESITATE TO CALL A LIE A LIE AND MOST OF ALL, DO NOT GIVE UP.

DISCUSSION QUESTIONS

STORY 1: RECOVERED

1. What are some of Josh's thoughts and feelings towards his father, Roman?
2. Is Josh's attitude and behavior toward his father warranted?
3. Given Josh's age of seventeen and his developmental stage in life, what are some of the ways he has likely been impacted by his father's history of addiction?
4. What are some other ways that Shelly and Josh can prepare for Roman's return from treatment?
5. What type of support do Shelly, Josh, and Roman require and how do they differ?
6. What expectations should Shelly and Josh have regarding Roman's recovery?
7. What understanding should Roman have regarding the impact of his relapses upon his family?
8. Is Shelly in denial about her husband's chances at sustaining recovery?
9. Why is Shelly supportive of her husband at this

stage, given their history? Would you be able to remain supportive under such circumstances?

10. How is it possible for a father to sacrifice the needs of his family and miss precious life milestones due to addiction?

11. Was Roman disinterested in being a husband and father?

12. What are some things that can help Roman's sustained recovery become more likely?

STORY 2: LOST

1. What are the different thoughts and feelings each family member experiences regarding Marco's sentencing? How and why do they differ?
2. Why does Gladys feel they have given up on their son? What more could she have done as a mother? What more could Gladys and Joel have done as parents, if anything?
3. If Marco has been incarcerated for some time and no longer experiencing symptoms of withdrawal, why are his cravings so strong?
4. Given the extensive consequences of his drug use, why is Marco still unable to address his actions and embrace sobriety?
5. What are some of the reasons why Marco is not feeling concerned with his family's reactions during his sentencing?
6. Does Gabi feel as if her family has emotionally neglected her over the years? If so, why and how?
7. Has Marco's family given up hope? Would you give

up hope if a family member repeatedly relapsed and faced incarceration?

8. Was Joel's decision not to find legal representation for his son justified?

9. If you were Judge Harris how would you sentence Marco?

10. Name some of the underlying reasons why Marco can put his family in jeopardy to obtain drugs?

11. Does Marco lack any empathy for others?

12. Is Marco's family correct in seeking counseling from a mental health expert? Given the advice they received, do you believe they reacted correctly when Marco made a request from them?

STORY 3: GONE

1. How is Tracy experiencing the loss of her daughter, Brittany?
2. What are some of Tracy's thoughts and feelings?
3. What are some of the ways Tracy could cope with her loss?
4. In your opinion, is Tracy's reaction to her losing her daughter "normal?" Is there a "right" way to react to such a profound loss?
5. Is it possible to overcome the grief Tracy is experiencing?
6. Given her close relationship with Brittany, what else could Tracy have done to help her daughter, if anything?
7. Was Brittany's letter to her mother sincere?
8. If Brittany really wanted to recover, why was she unable to follow through with the comments she related in her letter to Tracy?
9. Will Tracy ever be able to return to feeling herself again? What does the future hold for her?

NOTES

INTERESTED IN ADDICTION/RECOVERY SERVICES?

Now Offering:

- Online Recovery Coaching
- Online Recovery Group Coaching
- Sober Companion
- Sober Transport
- Intervention Services

For More Information or to Schedule a Consult:
Email: Coaching@BlakeEvanCohen.com
-Or-
Visit: BlakeEvanCohen.com

ABOUT THE AUTHOR

Blake Cohen began his career in the field of substance abuse treatment in his home state of Florida. Fueled by passion and gratitude for having overcome his own battles with addiction, he completed his bachelor's degree in psychology at Florida Atlantic University and earned a state certification as an Addictions Professional to better assist those struggling with substance use disorders. Blake wrote *I Love You, More* to offer perspective to family members – including the addict and their loved ones. Combining his personal and work experiences, along with many emotional interviews, he uses short, fictional stories to detail what a family unit endures when one of its members struggles with addiction. His two-fold goal is to combat the stigma surrounding the disease of addiction and educate those who are in the dark about it. The National Outreach Manager for Recovery Unplugged, a treatment center,

Blake currently lives with his wife, Chrissy, in Fort Lauderdale, FL.

If you would like to ask a question or share your thoughts regarding the book or your experience with addiction, email Blake at blake@blakeevancohen.com.

Interested in booking him as a speaker? Email booking@blakeevancohen.com.

Sign up for Blake's newsletter at www.blakeevancohen.com and receive a free gift, *10 Signs and Symptoms to Look for If You Suspect Your Loved One Has a Substance Use Disorder*.

If you'd like more information on Recovery Unplugged Treatment Centers, Blake's current place of employment, visit: www.ReadILoveYouMore.com.

RESOURCES

Treatment Resources
https://www.samhsa.gov

12-Step Family Support
https://al-anon.org or https://www.nar-anon.org

Alcoholics Anonymous
http://www.aa.org

Narcotics Anonymous
https://www.na.org

SMART Recovery
https://www.smartrecovery.org

Find a Therapist
https://www.psychologytoday.com/us

National Data
https://www.samhsa.gov/data/

Made in the USA
Columbia, SC
05 March 2020

88743522R00071